Leadership

Finding and Awaking The Young Leader In You

By

James C. Williams

My Opening Remarks

There is one amongst the many that will come forward as the one that came from the many....to lead them. - James Williams

Are you the one that came forward to lead the many? We have been waiting for a strong, good leader. We have been waiting for you. In this book, you will learn many different things, some funny, some interesting and all are about leadership and all have tremendous value. I want to be honest with you- Leadership is hard but it is necessary. Some leadership situations will be easier than others but, in many cases, you will be challenged from a personal perspective. True leadership is a challenge and it causes you to think about people and the project differently. For example, from a personal perspective, some people on your team may not like you even though you did nothing wrong to them or with the project. Some people will not like because of how you look, how you talk, or you will remind them of something negative in their past and they may never tell you about it. From a morale perspective, your actions and decisions can impact the morale of the team. Imagine that, someone is unhappy with you for making the right decision, but they didn't like it or agree with it. If you are too hard on them, they will not like you and if you are too easy on them, they will walk all over you and try to take advantage of you. You must find that balance of being firm and keeping them focused on the job. Lastly, as the leader, you are responsible for getting the project completed. Your team is supposed to do the work under your leadership so you must know the project and be able to direct actions and assign people to tasks. Some people may not want to do the work of the project or may seek to be a distraction to others. Regardless, you must stay focused on your job as leader. Do your job as the leader and during those difficult times, you must trust that you are doing your best despite their feelings or what they say. Please don't give up trying to be a good leader and continue to seek out other leadership opportunities- we need you.

This book is supposed to give an idea of what to expect as a leader and offer you tips to be a good leader. This book will not cover every situation you will encounter; however, it gives you some leadership lessons to help you with nearly any situation. This book is also designed to be your personal leadership guide which means you can write in this book the things you learn from reading this book, your personal experiences or your thoughts about something you read. After you finish reading the book, come back and look at what you wrote, and your thoughts.

Let's get started with a leadership poem. The poem talks about you and your team and the need for you to lead them. Chapter 1 focuses on the definition of leadership and the key parts of leadership. Chapter 1 also focuses on you as a person. Chapter 2 focuses on your Team. Your team are the ones doing the work and they can be a challenge, but you need to understand what to expect from the team. This book offers some insight into the team dynamics. Chapter 3 is a collection of leadership stories designed to make you think and reinforce what you learned in Chapters 1 and 2.

As a bonus, you will be presented with a series of questions to help you to reflect on what you learned throughout the book. Finally, at the very end, you will make a promise, your promise-to yourself. It is very powerful, and I don't suggest reading it until after you finished reading the entire book AND after you have read it with your parents. As your personal leadership diary, this book is yours, written for you, designed with you in mind and I hope it helps you in every part of your life.

Sincerely,

James C. Williams

Leadership

I want to do well
My heart and mind are in the right place
I'm prepared for the challenge
I'm about to face
As a leader,
I think about my team
They need me to be strong and firm
They need me to be kind and not mean
I think about the work
And what needs to be done today
I need to be organized
And assign tasks in a fair and smart way
I am not perfect
And neither is my team
I will do my best everyday
And I expect the same from my team
I don't need to be the leader
That I want to be
Rather, I need to be the leader
They need me to be
I need to lead them
To get the job done
Victory isn't declared
Until the we all have won
And the work is done...

By James Williams

CHAPTER 1
Leadership Defined
Key Parts of Leadership

Every decision you made in your life led you up to the moment of reading this book. - James Williams

Imagine yourself leading a small team of people, coed, around your same age and imagine yourself doing a great job of leading the team and completing the project correctly, ahead of schedule with no problems. Now, define leadership based upon what you just imagined. Leadership is defined differently by different people. It is defined differently by a young person and differently by a more mature person. If you ask 20 people from different backgrounds and different cultures to define leadership, you are likely to get over 20 different responses because leadership is uniquely defined by each person. In everyone's mind, they have an image of leadership and they have a definition of leadership based upon that image in their mind. Everyone's image and definition are slightly different because it is based upon the individual and their experiences. When YOU ask someone to define leadership, you instinctively compare their definition to the image and definition of leadership in your mind. Who is right and who is wrong? Both are right because the definition of leadership is based upon each person. Let's try it. In the space below, I want you to write down your definition of leadership, preferably without using the word leadership or lead.

My definition of leadership is:

_____

_____

Now, this is how I define leadership - The ability to influence people and influence the situation to get the desired outcome or job or task(s) accomplished. I didn't say you had to be the tallest, smartest or talk the loudest or be special in any way because once you read this book, you will have a better understanding of yourself, the characters on a team you lead and how to use your personal style leadership to get the work and project done.

3 Key Parts of Leadership

For the trip, each of the 3 friends did their part and they were so happy to celebrate their accomplishment as a team. - James Williams

Leadership has many parts and each part of leadership is equally as important as the other parts. I'm going narrow the parts of leadership down into 3 parts so we can focus on each part. The 3 Key parts to leadership are: You the leader, the team you are leading and the application of leadership or using leadership to get the work done and the project completed. Below you will find a very brief description for each and then we'll go deeper into each one:

1. You- You must understand yourself to include likes/dislikes and how you like to work. This will help you to understand why you want things done a certain and what you will require of others. By knowing yourself, it will help you to better understand the people you are leading and how you are leading them.
2. Team- They are doing the work and they need you to lead them plus it is your job as the leader. They need you to try and understand them, but they need for you to positively influence their behavior and guide their actions in an organized and focused manner. They

aren't perfect, you aren't perfect and nor are their lives which may impact their productivity.

3. Application or using your leadership skills- Using what you know about yourself, the project and your team to lead them. Later in this book, you will take what you learned from #1 and #2 and use it when you read the leadership stories. Think about how you might handle the situations as a leader. This includes having a positive relationship and understanding of your supervisor or boss.

You

Although mirrors don't lie, you can see and not see what you want in a mirror. - James Williams

In this section, we focus on two areas: you as a leader, and your leadership focus or your leadership pet peeves. Knowing yourself is the foundation of your leadership because your life and experiences will affect the decisions you make as a leader and why you want certain things done a certain way. It is all about you in leadership, and how you approach your leadership.

However, when we discuss leadership focus or leadership pet peeves, we are saying that there are certain things that every leader focuses their attention. Every leader is different, so each leader has their own areas of focus which influences how they lead their team. For example, being on time or strictly following rules or doing things at certain times are all examples of leadership focus or leadership pet peeves. It may have been an experience, or it just may be how they think but there are certain areas, that are personal to that leader, and it guides them as they lead. Enjoy this chapter because it is about you.

You as the Leader

I must ask you a question: "Are you a leader?" The answer is "yes" because everyone is a leader of at least one person-yourself. You lead yourself and everyday your behavior is influenced by your thoughts, your culture and what you have been taught. Your personal leadership skills are practiced daily, and you can almost argue that those that get into trouble a lot aren't practicing good self-leadership because it is influencing them to make bad or poor decisions for their life. You don't have to be named the team leader or be the loudest to be a leader and get the job done but you must understand yourself first. You are unique. There are many people in this world but only one you. As a leader, be yourself and be confident in being yourself and what you know. You are not perfect but try to be the best "you" that you can be. When I started thinking about being the best me and leadership, I was in the Navy, in my 20's and I realized I wanted to make the Navy my career. I realized that I needed to do better all phases of my life from education, doing a better job at work, and being a better leader. I don't want you to wait until your 20s to start thinking about leadership and thinking about understanding yourself and being the best you. I want you to start now. Part of understanding yourself is figuring out why you like or do certain things. For me, I tried to understand why I like certain things or like doing things a certain way. I found out that I love for things to be done in a logical manner because it is easier for me to remember the steps. Also, it is easier for me to explain processes that are logical to someone new so they can understand the process. Now, when I am the leader of a project, I try to make sure my decisions and processes are logical.

Sometimes, thinking about ourselves more deeply as a leader can be difficult because we don't know where to start. To assist, I have created a series of questions designed to get you think about yourself and yourself as a leader. Also, these questions will help you to get to know yourself. Remember, in your mind, you have an image of a leader but when you answer these questions, I'm asking about YOU not the leader in your mind nor am I looking for a "perfect" answer. Your answers will be perfect and correct because your responses are unique for you. If leadership starts with you, then we need to think about how you would view leadership and leadership situations. Be honest when answer these questions as this book is your personal leadership diary. The answers are yours and you are welcome to change them as you read this book, but I want you to be honest with yourself as you answer these questions. You can skip some questions, but I want you to come back and answer them by the end of the book.

Getting To Know Myself Questions

Do you prefer to work alone or with a team or group?

_____

Do you prefer being the leader of a group or just a member of a group and not the leader?

_____

If you were offered to lead a team, would you accept the offer or refuse the offer and why?

_____

Do you like to plan then start work or start working and adjust as needed?

_____

Do you know what makes you happy when you work on a project with a team?

_____

Do you know what makes you frustrated when working on project with a team?

_____

How do you adjust to changes when the situation or project changes?

_____

What do you think about when you have to work with people from different cultures or races on a project?

_____

What is your approach to solving problems with a project?

_____

Are you good at figuring out people's talent or skills to determine what they are good and no-so- good at when working on a project?

_____

Would you prefer to lead a team of girls or boys or coed and why?

_____

The last time you were the leader on a project, do you remember it going well or not-so well and why?

_____

Do you enjoy teaching something new to someone?

_____

Do you have a problem with assigning people a job or task?

_____

Most people don't ask themselves or think about the questions above when they think about leadership. Knowing about yourself impacts the way you define leadership and how you will lead others. As you get more experiences, there may be a natural evolution of your thoughts, behaviors and understanding and your application of leadership.

Leadership Focus

Different leaders focus on different things- in the picture above, some focus on the eyes, some focus on the color, and some focus on the spots...of a jaguar! - James Williams

Leadership focus or leadership pet peeves is unique for each leader, and it is part of knowing yourself. Leadership focus are those things that every leader tends to focus on as they are leading people. For example, some leaders really focus on punctuality or being on time while some may focus on deadlines or communication. They focus on their leadership pet peeves because this is what they feel comfortable focusing on or something they experienced caused them to focus on this. If you have an experience of being on time but having peers whose tardiness negatively impacts the jobs, then as a leader, your focus may be expressing the need to be on time. You may become frustrated with people who are often tardy. Time and punctuality are probably important to you. Again, this is unique for each leader and yours may be totally different. Some leaders focus on feedback and communication. They want to know about everything, every detail or problem or issue about the project as soon as possible. This isn't wrong, but this is their leadership focus and it is important to them. A leader isn't wrong for having these unique things they focus on; however, they need to communicate to their team about these areas. This will help the team to better understand you as the leader and to focus on the things that you are focused on. The more you serve in leadership roles, the more you will know and understand the things you will focus on. You may have one or more than one. For me, I want the process followed exactly how it is supposed to be done and I want communication from me and to me to be clear. These are important to me because if something happens, I will be able to follow the process to see where the breakdown occurred, and I want to know what is working and what isn't working. Take a moment to write down some of the areas you may focus on as a leader and provide your reason(s) why:

Your Leadership focus area
#1:_____

Reason(s):_____

Your Leadership focus area
#2:_____

Reason(s):_____

Your Leadership focus area
#3:_____

Reason(s):_____

<u>Summary</u>

You are the first part of the 3 key parts of leadership. Therefore, you need to understand yourself, and know that you are unique. You need to know what things you will focus on as a leader. Remember, you aren't perfect, and you don't have to be perfect in order to be a good leader. You will have some areas of improvement but that doesn't stop you from being a good person and a good leader. In Chapter 2, we will focus on the 2nd key part of leadership- The Team. Now, imagine yourself leading a small team of people, coed, around your same age and imagine yourself doing a great job of leading them, completing the project ahead of schedule with no problems.

__Chapter 2__

The Team

Some great teams are often made up of different people from different backgrounds. - James Williams

Your team are the people doing the work. Please don't ever forget that. You need them. The work or project must get done and the team, with you leading them, will get it done. However, each team member has a mind and life of their own that they bring with them to the project. Sometimes, this may conflict with others. Based upon my experience, there are 3 major tips I'm going to share about the team. They are the characters/roles, communication and focusing their energy.

3 Major Tips about the Team

Tip# 1- The 4 Main Characters on a team

The Lion, Wolf, Sheep and Lamb are the 4 characters or roles of players on your team and we discuss how they tend to behave. These characteristics are not designed to put people in a stereotypical role rather it generally defines their behavioral characteristics. They may move between different roles sometimes in the same day. These roles should not prevent you from giving them a fair chance for any opportunity.

Tip# 2- Communication

How do you share information on your team? Information is precious and everyone needs it. They need to know what to do, when do it, and how you want it done. They need to know about changes and how changes impact what they are doing and the project. Don't take communication for granted and assume someone else will do it or they should already know.

Tip# 3- Focusing their energy

Focusing their energy- Keep them focused on the project and working on the project. There may be a little down time but minimize it. People who are working should have little time to play around and get distracted. Keep them focused on the work which means you or your leadership style can't be a distraction to the team and don't let poor communication distract or negatively impact their productivity.

TIP# 1
4 Characters on a Team

Work together to create something-like hearts. - James Williams

The team consists of different people from different backgrounds. Often, people bring their background and experiences to work. Their background and experiences are expressed in different ways, most of the time it is positive, sometimes it is negative. As a leader, you must understand the characters on your team. People may start out in one character but end up in another character sometimes in the same day. The characters are based upon the behavior of the individual. As a leader, you must be able to recognize these characters and influence their behavior to get the project done. The goal would be for everyone to be themselves unless they are a Wolf.

4 Characters on a Team

Lion

<u>Positive-</u> Has leadership skills, future leader, seeks to do well and work well with others.

<u>Negative-</u> Wants to be in charge and may seek to take control of a small group or worse may seek to take your position as leader.

Wolf

<u>Positive-</u> They can be a fun distraction from the grind of work for a very short time.

<u>Negative-</u> Seeks to disrupt, distract, not always using energy for good.

Sheep

<u>Positive-</u> Hard workers, seek to give their best and want to do well. Some can be converted to a Lion.

<u>Negative-</u> They can be a little stubborn to small changes and especially stubborn when there are major changes. If not properly guided, they can be converted to a Wolf.

Lamb

<u>Positive-</u> Hard workers, fresh energy, will seek your feedback and approval. Lots of potential if properly guided by you. You will see the future in them before they see it in themselves.

<u>Negative-</u> They are easily distracted, at times they want to be distracted, and can be easily distracted by a Wolf and converted to a Wolf, needs a lot of attention and direction.

Lion

The Lion has leadership skills and they have the potential to be a leader. They may try to lead every project and the people. Their intentions are usually good but if you are leader, then you need to make sure the Lion doesn't take your leadership position. They may be seen by others as a leader, which is fine, but again make sure you use them to help the team and project but not take over your project. Eventually, the Lion will get their chance to lead but don't let them take your opportunity to lead. Secretly, select one or more of the Lion as your "friend" on the team. They will be the person that you can talk to about different things as their feedback may be very helpful. You don't have to tell them they are your "friend", but you will need to have someone that watches your back and understand what you are going through as the leader. The Lion can be a girl or boy and your "friend" can be a girl or boy.

Wolf

The Wolf seeks to disrupt, distract, and NOT always use their talent, skills or energy for good. This doesn't mean they are bad people on the inside as I'm referring to their behavior. They may be good people, but the Wolf may not be aware they are a Wolf and how their behavior negatively impacts the project. Sometimes, they may be confused with a Lion because of the attention they are getting, people may think they are a leader. People may like being around them and they may be friendly, but they keep people from working on the project. They may be talented, and you need their talent and skills to work on the project, but you need to keep an eye on them, and ensure they are working on the project. You may have one or two of them on your team. If they can work together, that's fine, but sometimes they feed off each other and they encourage poor behavior from the other. Keep the Wolf busy working on the project. The Wolf can be a girl or boy.

Sheep

The Sheep can be a little stubborn as it relates to changes, but they usually are players that work very hard and give you little or no problems. However, as with any team member, they can be a converted into a Lion or Wolf. The Sheep typically seeks to use their energy for good and they will seek to help you and others on the project. Since major changes or too many small changes implemented too quickly tend to frustrate them, make sure you seek their input on changes to the project or process and especially involve them in the implementation of any changes. Make sure they know about any changes well in advance. Most of your players will fall into this group. A frustrated Sheep can become a Wolf as they will tend to draw attention to themselves or an issue that is not easily solvable. The Sheep can be a girl or boy.

Lamb

A Lamb is a person who is easily distracted or is a younger version of a sheep. You will see their potential, but they will not nor are they seeking to their potential. Don't get frustrated with them as they are still learning about working and themselves. You may want to pair them up with a Lion or Sheep. They will seek to use energy for good unless they are being distracted. They may need more attention and direction than the others. They want to have a good time and they may see work as a chore. You will need them to do their part on the project. Perhaps setting small goals for them to work towards will help keep them focused. Ideally, you want them to work hard on the project and grow up to be a Sheep or Lion. The Wolf loves Lambs because they give the Wolf the attention they want and need which is used to distract others. The Lambs can be a girl or boy.

Now that you have read about the 4 characters on a team, I know want you to look at the groups of people in your life and complete the analysis below. In the space below, I want you to write down at least 3 groups or teams you are a part of and/or know about and I want you to answer the questions. See the example below and then complete the next three.

EXAMPLE:

Group name: 6th grade homeroom

Number of people: 25 students, mixture of boys and girl. 13 girls and 12 boys.

Number of Lions: 5

Number of Wolves: 2

Number of Sheep: 15

Number of Lambs: 3

Explanation: The class is full of good students but there is one boy and one girl that behave in a way that draws a lot of attention from the teacher and from the class for no other reason than to get attention.

Now, you try it. Again, I'm not looking for perfect answers, rather I want you to think about the groups or teams you are surrounded by and pick out the 4 different characters. Remember, you can have a team or group with all sheep if that is what you observe. Your turn…

Identifying Characters in your group 1

Group Name:

Number of people:

Number of Lions:

Number of Wolves:

Number of Sheep:

Number of Lambs:

Explanation:_____

_____

Identifying Characters in your group 2

Group Name:

Number of people:

Number of Lions:

Number of Wolves:

Number of Sheep:

Number of Lambs:

Explanation:_____

_____

<u>Identifying Characters in your group 3</u>

Group-

Number of people:

Number of Lions:

Number of Wolves:

Number of Sheep:

Number of Lambs:

Explanation:_____

_____

TIP# 2
Communication

Everyone talks about communication, but it is seldom practiced. - James Williams

Communication is foundation of leadership. Poor communication can negatively influence your team moral, attitude, and productivity. Communication isn't just talking and saying things without thinking about them. As a leader, your words and behavior are forms communication and you should use them to guide your team mentally and their actions to where you want them to go. However, you don't have to be robot and be so focused on the project, but you need to ensure what you say, you mean and that it helps and not hurt. No gossiping and no talking bad about your team to other team members. Those are just the basics but there are 3 key things you need know for communication. In addition, we will discuss how to handle conflicts or conflict resolution. This will be very helpful because conflicts will arise on every team. For now, let's focus on the 3 Communication Tips.

Communication Tip#1

First, you need to make sure they understand what you are saying so you need to say things in a logical, succinct way and use proper details and examples that matter to them. This will help them to pay attention, listen and remember.

Communication Tip#2

Second, they need to understand their role or their part. This is very similar to the first one, but it is different. The first tip advises you on how and what to say, the second tip is telling you to make sure each player understands their role and what they are supposed to be doing. If you don't communicate this clearly and often, they will tend to do what they think is right and it may not be what you want them to do.

Communication Tip#3

Third, they need to understand the project and how the project is supposed to look at the end. They need to understand how they contribute to the larger project. For example, there may be several parts and pieces to the project and they will be connected or put together at the very end. The player needs to know how it will look in the end, why it is important to do a good job and most importantly, they need to know if any delays on their part negatively impacts others or the large project. This is very important.

__Handling of conflicts__

Not if but when conflicts arise and when conflicts will arise, will you arise to situation and resolve the conflicts? – James Williams

Conflicts are disagreements or issues between you and one or more of your players or between two or more players. Conflicts are common, nearly every team has conflicts. Don't be afraid of conflicts and don't go overboard trying to prevent them or solve them. Teach your team about conflict resolution in advance and often. Teach them about how to handle conflicts and teach them how to bring conflicts to your attention. With any conflict, always listen, ask lots of questions and be thinking about the resolution. The resolution doesn't always have to involve major changes, it can be as simple as you listening to both parties and allowing them to listen to the other person. Be sure to ask the players involved, what do they think a fair resolution should be? Don't let their emotions or your emotions sway your feedback or decisions. Be guided by the truth, the facts and logic. Think about how you want to see this resolved now and, if there is a next time. Ask for help and guidance from your leader if needed. You are not alone and don't allow your decision(s) or how they feel about your decision serve as a wedge or divider on the team. See if you can influence the situation in a positive way to keep the work on the project going and not be delayed or negatively impacted.

TIP# 3
Focus their Energy

Even a kitten can stop playing and focus for one moment. - James Williams

Life is about energy and focus and so focus their energy and attention on the work of the project. The team will have a lot of energy, but unfocused energy can lead to chaos, time-wasting and no or very little productivity on the project. Remember, you have work to do on the project and if the team/players aren't given directions to focus their energy, you may lose control of your team. When you lose control of the team, there is a chance you may lose your role as the leader of the team. Focusing their energy on the project doesn't mean there won't be moments of laughter and fun, but the team needs to be kept focused on their part and the overall project. You can use these 3 tips below:

1. Create a theme or goals (Vision/Mission) they are working towards.
2. Show their progress.
3. Create cross-training goals.

Vision and Mission

Vision is where we are going, and the Mission are the steps you take every day to get you there. - James Williams

Vision and Mission are fancy words adults and companies use to describe how they want to be known and what they are doing. You want to keep these simple and repeatable and you want to remind your team often about the mission. The mission is supposed to accomplish the vision.

Here is an example of Vision and Mission statements: If you were making toy castles to donate to nonprofit agencies and they gave those toys to kids that live in homeless shelters. So, if you are making castles then your vision statement may be "To be known as a team that makes high quality castles for good causes". Your mission statement may be like "To make high quality castles to be donated to nonprofit agencies that help kids.". The mission is what you do every day to accomplish the vision. To keep it simple, take the title of the project and create your mission first because that is what you are trying to do each day. The vision is how you want your team to be know when they accomplish the mission.

Let's let you try to write a mission and vision statement.

Purpose: Picking oranges to donate to a food bank

Mission:_____

_____

Vision:_____

_____

Let's try again.....

Purpose: Filling sandbags for local County to give out during floods.

Mission:

_____

_____

Vision:_____

_____

Their progress = our progress

Progress is knowing that your hard work is getting you one step closer to accomplishing your goal. You may know but they may not know unless you show them and tell them- James Williams

Showing progress and connecting your team to their progress is very important. It means that their work isn't in vain or not being noticed. People learn 3 different ways like listening, hearing and seeing. If they learn these ways, then you can connect their progress the same 3 ways. Keep it simple, you can have a chart that shows the progress to what you are trying to accomplish. Use this tool to speak to it for the auditory learners. The ones that connect through doing will see their progress.

Cross-training as a goal

Once you learn one instrument, start learning another one so that you can make music with any instrument available. - James Williams

Cross-training is simply teaching your team to do more than one thing, so they can be an additional asset to the team. Basically, if you have a player who only does one thing and doesn't know how to do anything else, if someone is out then it can negatively impact the team's productivity and the project. You need to be able to do and teach everyone's part as the leader, so you need to be cross-trained and have a good understanding. Keep the cross-training simple, you don't have to make it a large project. For example, if you are making toy houses and you use the assembly line approach, well one player is only gluing on doors, they need to know how to set up the base of the toy house or put on windows. This is example is very simplistic, so you get the idea of cross-training. Again, as the leader, you need to know everyone's job and be able to either have someone partner with another player to get cross-trained or you may need to cross-training them.

CHAPTER 3
Leadership Stories

Finally, we are here at the 3rd key part of leadership. It is using the tips from 1st and 2nd key parts of leadership. Here are some leadership stories for you to read slowly and think about. There is a place after each story for you to share your thoughts, for example, if you want to identify different characters, discuss the lessons and what do you THINK you would have done. Each story is unique with different lessons and things for you think about.

LEADERSHIP STORY #1
Accepting the Challenge

Be strong, control your fear and go for it.- James Williams

At school, the class was divided up into teams to work on a class project. Each team consists of 5 people, and there are girls and boys on the team. Each team must select a leader from among the 5 people and the goal is to build a wooden stage that is strong and mobile. One of the 5 people is a girl named Mary. After asking everyone who wants to be the team leader, Mary volunteered, and the team voted her in as the team leader. Mary knew it was going to be a challenge, but she felt confident enough to be the team leader and help her team complete the project.

Leadership Lesson: Be confident in yourself, accept the challenge of being a team leader, do your best and learn from your experience.

Your thoughts:

_____

_____

LEADERSHIP STORY #2
Afraid of being in charge

Fear, the internal belief that you should be afraid- what if you ignored it or didn't believe that. – James Williams

At school, Pam was on a book club team and one of the positions on the team was the team leader. The team leader would serve for a semester. Their duties included presenting several books for the team to choose from and then select a day for the class to talk about the book and lead the discussion points. She had been on the team since last year because she loved to read, and her favorite book was "Happy Cakes" by James Williams. It seemed logical that Pam would volunteer to be the leader of the group. Pam didn't because she afraid the kids would think and say bad things about her if she picked books that weren't good or interesting. The team asked Pam to be the leader and she respectfully declined.

Leadership Lesson: Leadership is hard but necessary and when we don't accept the challenge, everyone misses out on learning from you and you missed out on the opportunity to teach others and learn about yourself.

Your thoughts:

_____

_____

LEADERSHIP STORY #3
Not prepared, not organized

As a leader, your mind and your team' actions must be as organized as this desk. Disorganization leads to chaos, wasted time and lack of productivity. - James Williams

At school, the principal was putting together a team to paint and decorate the float for the local parade. He had about 20 people who volunteered and a few of them were on the team last year. Daisy asked the principal could she be the leader of the decorating team and the principal selected her as the team leader. Daisy called an after-school meeting to discuss the details. At the meeting, Daisy kept referring to how much fun it was last year, and who liked who. The team was wondering when she was going to get to their decorating project. She didn't have any notes and talked about everything from paint, colors, supplies but none of it made sense. The team left the meeting not knowing what they were supposed to do or the next steps.

Leadership Lesson: As the leader, you must be organized when you work with a team and have a plan of action. Don't waste the teams' time and energy on things that aren't part of the project or important to the project.

Your thoughts:

_____

_____

LEADERSHIP STORY #4
Leadership focus

Leadership focus- Name any two things in this picture that you focused on first, everyone else focused on two different things like the time and the glasses. - James Williams

Julie was a smart young lady, she was served on the honor roll party team for her first 2 years in high school. This year, she was selected as the team leader of the party planning committee. At the meeting, she asked for ideas for the party. Her team of 10 people had plenty of ideas to share with the group. However, when they presented them, Julie would interject to correct the way they presented it constantly telling them they were starting in the middle instead of the beginning. Also, she kept asking them "About how much do you think that would cost?". The meeting quickly turned negative and others began to be afraid to speak up out of fear of someone being critical of an idea of a brainstorming session.

Leadership Lesson: As a leader, you need to be clear with your communication about what you want and expect from people. If you don't tell them what you want, how can you expect them to know?

Your thoughts:

_____

_____

LEADERSHIP STORY #5
Dealing with the Wolf

At the local taco shop, there was a girl named Bridget that worked the afternoon shift after school and on weekends. She was a hard worker and her manager noticed that she was always on time and made very few mistakes with any of the orders. She was very quick at understanding complicated orders and she was a great teammate to new employees by helping them and training them. The manager decided to make her a shift leader. On that afternoon shift was another girl, Angela, who didn't like that fact that Bridget was selected over her. She decided to give Bridget a hard time and to get others to not listen to make Bridget look bad in the eyes of her manager. She was successful in her efforts until Bridget caught on to what she was doing. Bridget, understanding that not everyone is going to like you as a leader, took swift action. She pulled Angela into a quick meeting to discuss her actions. She documented the discussion topics of the meeting and informed Angela that if it continued, she was going to inform the manager. She told Angela what the expectations were and that she wanted to work with Angela not against her. After the meeting, Angela pulled all the shift workers together, including Angela, and reminded them about appropriate behavior and how inappropriate behavior negatively impacted the work and the customer.

Leadership lesson: Don't wait to deal with a Wolf, have a plan to deal with them and be decisive. Document discussions and document all issues. Ensure everyone is reminded about your standards of conduct, and how their conduct or behavior may impact others and the work. Keep your manager informed of these types of situations.

Your thoughts:

_____

_____

LEADERSHIP STORY #6
Leader trying to take over

At Katie's school, they were going to decorate the halls to recognize all the kids at her school who made honor role. The teachers on that hall asked which students want to participate and help decorate the walls. Out of 10 classrooms on that hallway, 25 kids total volunteered to assist. The most senior teacher had to select a leader of the project, so she selected Katie. The teacher knew Katie as she had her in one of her classes, and Katie was an honor roll student with no behavior or conduct problems at school. Out of the 25 kids, there was another student that wanted to lead the group and his name was Tom. Tom was in the same grade as Katie and his school record was very similar to Katie's. Tom approached Katie and the teacher to ask if he could be Katie's Assistant Leader. Everyone agreed that they could use Tom's help in that role, and they divided the remaining students into two groups and put Tom in charge of one group and Katie in charge of the other group while Katie remained in charge of the entire project. Everyone knew Katie oversaw the entire project. During one of the scheduled decorating days, Katie was running late to the hall. As she was walking to the hallway, she walked past a classroom that had many of the student volunteers in her group and she saw Tom standing at the front of the class. She wondered why they were there since she hadn't scheduled a meeting and she wondered why the students from her group were at Tom's meeting. She slowly turned around and walked slowly back to the classroom. As she was walking back, she could hear Tom's voice saying things and totally changing the things she had told them to do. She could hear him telling the students to come to see him if they had questions. As she reached the door of the classroom, and when Tom saw her, he immediately ended the meeting. As the students filed past her, some of them looked a little confused about what had happened. Katie stopped one of the kids in her group and quickly asked her "What's going on in here?". They told her Tom had passed out a flyer and told them to meet with him for some announcements. She spoke with Tom after everyone had left and he made it seem like it was no big deal that he called a meeting without telling her and he was making a "few" changes to some of her decisions.

Leadership lesson: As a leader, it is good to have an assistant or co-leader but if you are the leader, you can't delegate your responsibility. You are the leader. Others can help but they should not be viewed as the leader. Keep watch for people on your team who are trying to take your position as leader.

Your thoughts:

_____

_____

LEADERSHIP STORY #7
Sheep converted to Lion
(Encouraging people in non-leadership positions to take a leadership role)

While in her leadership class, Dia learned about the Lion, Wolf, Sheep and Lamb. She tried to see if she saw those characters amongst the 11 staff members at the local animal shelter that she worked at on weekends. She was a shift leader and she need an assistant shift leader. While observing the staff, she saw the four characters being played out but one thing that really made her take notice was the person named Paula who wasn't in a leadership role, but they seemed to know how to do everything at the shelter. Paula would be seen teaching the new staff and volunteers about the shelter. Although Paula never inquired about the assistant shift leader position, Dia felt like this person could probably be a great assistant shift leader and help her run the entire team and shift. She approached Paula, and she accepted the opportunity to be a leader.

Leadership lesson: You want to encourage your team to do their best and help them to be young leaders.

Your thoughts:

_____

_____

LEADERSHIP STORY #8
Lamb converted to Wolf

Julie was a junior in high school and it just so happened she was in the same gym class as a freshman named Sarah. Julie typically didn't get in trouble but started hanging around the wrong kids. She was hanging around kids who thought getting in trouble was and being rebellious made you popular. Although the school and her parents had spoken with her, she continued to hang around the wrong kids and do things to draw attention to herself. Lately, in gym class, she refused to dress out and when she would, she would purposely not follow directions. Sarah was a freshman who tried to do the right thing, but she really wanted to be cool and popular. Since she was in high school, she really thought being cool and popular was the best. Those thoughts drew her to Julie in the gym class. She thought she was so cool when she didn't dress out and she thought Julie was tough when she refused to follow directions when she dressed out. Sarah would purposely stand near Julie when they were in line playing a game or went outside. Sarah would ask Julie about the wrong things she did and how was she able to get away with it. They soon became friends with Julie being like a cool big sister to Sarah. Sarah was so impressed that she thought she would try not dressing out to get attention class and be popular amongst the kids at school.

Leadership lesson: Lambs are easy targets for the Wolf. Wolves love Lambs because they give them the attention they need and want. Keep the lambs away from the wolves.

Your thoughts:

_____

_____

LEADERSHIP STORY #9
Finding a "Friend"

Find friends that will be by your side on your best and worst days. – James Williams

Leyla was on the high school debate team. She was logical, organized and had a passion for debate. She loved taking her opponents' ideas or words and using them against to win the debate. She did so well on the debate that when she was a sophomore in high school, they asked her to be the President of the debate team. She had the most wins, she understood how to prepare, and she worked well with others on team in preparation. Leyla got along well with nearly everyone on the team, however, there a few upper classmen, boys and girls, that didn't like that a sophomore was selected over them. They tried to work together against Leyla, however, there was one that Leyla really liked as a debater and as a friend and her name was Donna. Donna was a senior and although she was a good, she didn't think she was as good as Leyla. Leyla and Donna became friends over lunch and learned from each other. Because Donna believed and supported Leyla, she talked with the upperclassmen about their behavior towards Leya. She wanted them to understand that attacking someone on your team wasn't being a good teammate and it didn't help the team when they were competing against other debate clubs.

Leadership Lesson: Being a leader is hard, but it is necessary, and you need at least one good friend for support. Don't think you are in it alone.

Your thoughts:

_____

_____

LEADERSHIP STORY #10
Conflict Resolution

It is not a matter of if but when you have conflicts and when you have conflicts, no one is a happy kitty. - James Williams

Tonya was a junior editor on the high school yearbook. She took her job very seriously because she knew the impact of the yearbook. Seniors used the book as way to collect their senior memories, and others used the book as a way of documenting who went to high school with them. Also, she knew the yearbook was expensive, costing over $60. She wanted to make sure it was a good product that was worth the cost and was a precious memory for the seniors. There was the sports section that she assigned to Nicole and Rachel to take the pictures and organize them in a cool way. Nicole and Rachel decided to do everything together from going to the game, taking the pictures and organizing them in the yearbook format. Well, Nicole felt like she took the most pictures and she was doing the most work organizing the pictures. Plus, she wanted the sports to go in a certain order like spring sports then fall sports while Rachel wanted the sports to go in a different order. Rachel wanted the most popular sport, soccer, to go first followed by the smaller individual sports. This disagreement caused them to argue and request from Tonya to work on a different section of the yearbook. Tonya knew everyone was too far along to stop and start changing jobs. Plus, to pull someone from another project to work on the sports section would be cause additional delays on a project that was time-sensitive. She asked Nicole and Rachel to meet her afterschool at the local diner to discuss the project and their differences. She wrote down in advance of the meeting all the reasons why she didn't want to move them to another section of the yearbook. Tonya met them at the diner with Nicole showing up about 5 mins before Rachel. Once everyone was there, everyone talked about school and grades. Then, Tonya proceeded to the reasons why they were there. She laid out the project, and the assigned roles. She told them how long they had to complete the first draft and she told them the impact of not meeting that deadline. She stressed to them why the yearbook was so important. Tonya then asked Nicole to share her side of the disagreement, making notes about the project and differences. Tonya then asked Rachel to share her side of the story, again making notes about the project and the situation. Tonya was able to get them to agree on staying together on the same project and they ensured the work was as evenly divided as possible.

Leadership lesson: Anticipate conflicts and try to prevent them. If you know of a conflict, gather as much facts, and think of a reasonable solution then approach the individuals involved to get their side of the story and seek to work towards a reasonable solution.

Your thoughts:

_____
_____

LEADERSHIP STORY #11
Understanding your boss

Know your boss and make sure you know what they expect from you and their leadership focus. - James Williams

Kelly worked part-time on the weekends at the shipping company. The company shipped all sorts of boxes and supplies all over the world. Kelly worked in the warehouse and loved driving the forklift. Her Supervisor, Edna, thought Kelly was a great worker and she trusted her judgement. Kelly often went to Edna with new ideas or how to organize things differently to make them more efficient. Edna always took the time to listen to Kelly's ideas, and she incorporated several of them which saved the company some money and saved time processing the orders.

Leadership lesson: Every leader has a supervisor or boss, so you need to do a few things: establish a positive trusting relationship with your boss, seek advice from them on a variety of topics and seek guidance from them regarding the job you are doing.

Your thoughts:

_____

_____

LEADERSHIP STORY #12
You are a Role Model

You are a role model and you never know who is watching. Your behavior is being watched and modeled by others who want to be just like you. Even role models have role models. – James Williams

Jennifer worked in a grocery store after school. She worked in the produce section with 2 other people, Jeff and John, from her high school and she was the shift leader. Their job was to organize the backroom of fruit and vegetables so that the oldest came out first and put on the shelves. They had to keep the back area clean and make sure the fruit and vegetables were arranged in a neat way on the display table. Over a few weeks, Jennifer started to eat a few grapes as she was working to put them out on display. Then she started eating an apple or two and taking a few home when her shift ended. She didn't notice her other 2 coworkers were watching her, so they started to do the same thing except they were taking bunches of bananas, and several of the kiwi and oranges. One day as the manager was sitting in the upper office watching the video security camera, she noticed Jeff putting apple in his pocket. He approached Jeff about it and Jeff immediately told the manager he only did it because he saw Jennifer do it and figured it was ok.

Leadership lesson: Your people are watching what you do so watch what you do. Don't do anything that you don't want them to do.

Your thoughts:

_____
_____

TIME TO REFLECT

Make time to think about things, no music, no outside noise, just you thinking about the things in your life and thinking about yourself and your future. - James Williams

In this book, we have covered many things about leadership. Some of the things we covered, you may have never heard before or some of the things may have been presented differently. Regardless, I want you to take a moment to think about what you have learned from this book and how you can use it in your life. There are two areas in this section that I want to you to do. First, there are some questions for you to answer. These questions are just to help you to retain all the information you have learned and to see how you will use it in your life. My second request is your personal leadership letter for you to read, and sign. It your personal commitment to yourself as a young leader and as a person. You don't have to sign but I am asking you to read it. I think you will find it very encouraging as you get older and get more experience. It is a reminder to be strong, be brave and understand how to approach different situations.

Leadership Self Test
What did I learn and how will I use what I learned?

1. What did you find most interesting about this book?

a. _____

2. What did you find least interesting about this book?

a. _____

3. Name at least one lesson or tip you learned that you

    can use right now?

a. _____

4. If you were to share a lesson or tip with a friend, which

    one would it be and why?

a. _____

5. Based upon this book, will you volunteer to be a leader

    of a small project soon and why?

a. _____

6. Which part of leadership did you like, and you think you

    will use and why?

a. _____

7. What is your leadership focus, and do you know why?

   a. _____

8. What are the key parts of leadership?

   a. _____

9. How many different characters are there on a team and who are they?

   a. _____

10. What did you learn about yourself after reading this book?

   a. _____

Please write down any of your other thoughts:

_____

_____

_____

_____

_____

_____

My Promise

It is time to get a little more serious about you and your personal commitment to your personal growth as a person and to your growth as a young leader. Below is your promise to yourself. This promise is not to be taken lightly. I suggest you read it slowly at least 3 times before making the promise. When you AND your parents feel comfortable with it, please proceed to making your personal promise.......

I Promise
By James Williams

I, _____, understand that leadership is
Put Your Name
hard, but it is necessary. It is necessary for the success in my personal life and it is necessary for any team I'm on. I know that I may not be the person named the leader, but I am still a leader and my behavior can influence the team's attitude and behavior and it can impact the productivity of the team. I know leaders come in all sizes, shapes, ages, genders and colors. I may not be the biggest, strongest, fastest or smartest, but I will not let anyone outwork me. I promise to give my all and my best all the time. I promise to try and understand myself more. I will know my leadership focus areas. I will know the things that are important to me as I work as part of a team and I will try to know my strengths and weaknesses. As a strong, brave person, I'm willing to accept the right leadership challenges for me. I promise to make every effort to study the project and be knowledgeable or I will be an involved, productive member of any team I'm on. I promise to be as organized as I can and be

flexible with changes. I know the only constant in life is change so I expect changes to happen. I promise to listen and learn as much as I can from my family, friends, and other leaders. I promise to try my best in every situation even if it isn't the best situation. As a willing role model, I know others are watching what I do, and I promise to do the best I can but I'm not perfect and mistakes are a part of life. I promise to learn lessons from my mistakes and use them to move forward in a positive manner and I hope the person watching me will do the same. I understand that the people I may lead or work with may not look like me or share my background, but I will not let that be a barrier to our shared success. I promise to make every effort to practice good listening skills and be mindful of how my words affect people and situations. I promise to try and learn about and from other cultures to increase my awareness of other people and the world. I promise to make time to reflect upon my life, my decisions and my future. I promise to seek natural happiness in nature and find joy in small things and in my family. I promise every step of my personal plan will be carefully guided so I can be one step closer towards the personal goals in my life with the understanding that I must work hard for everything. I must earn it and I promise to not let disappointment or others distract me from my life's plan. I promise to control my emotions and convert my emotions to passion, so I'm focused on something positive not the negativity of the situation. As I make this promise to myself, I will remember that leadership is hard but necessary and I promise to never give up on myself and the belief that I can make a difference in this world.

Signed,

_____

Date: _____

Thank you for reading my book. I hope you enjoyed it, I hope you learned some lessons that you can use in your life and I hope you remember the right lessons at the right time and use them in the right way.

SPECIAL THANKS TO....

Thank you to my beautiful wife Amanda for your love and support through this dream. I love you.

Thank you to Dorothy for the being the strong young lady that you have always been. I love you.

Thank you to James for trying to be the best young man in every part of your life. I love you.

Thank you to Samantha for being the sweet, strong lady in my life. I love you.

Thank you to Blaze for being a thinker and being a great young man. I love you.

Special thanks to website unsplash.com who provided nearly all the photos in this book.

My other books you may enjoy:

All available on Amazon, however, if you want a signed copy order off my website: coachjames.org

Coach James Top Coaching Tips- A great book on how to coach kids, work with parents and help kids with life skills.

Happy Cakes- A young love story that is family-friendly, and authentic. It can be read in public, schools, and places of faith. There are many life lessons in this book.

My website: coachjames.org
Email: coachjamesbiz1@gmail.com

Letter to my Adult Readers

Dear Adult Reader,

Before you read this book, I wanted to forewarn you about a few things. First, this leadership book was written for kids/teens girls not for adults. Although you will find many of the same lessons that you will find in an adult leadership book, the leadership lessons here are written in a way for young people to think about and understand. Remember, their leadership experience is different from most adults. In addition, because of the content in this book, your leadership experience or education may be challenged by new concepts, thoughts or ideas presented in this book.

Second, you may learn something you didn't know before or you may think about something that you didn't think about before. If you try to read this book from your matured leadership perspective, you will find yourself time-traveling between your youth and your young adult life to your current self. This book is brilliantly written so that when an adult reads it, they are taken back to when they were a child or as a young adult and may have had a leadership experience. You may ponder that experience and wonder what you could or would have done differently had you read this book before that experience.

Lastly, as you know, there are many lessons you can learn about leadership and many scenarios to highlight those lessons. Since this book is designed to cover the foundation of leadership and to give them some tips, it will not cover every possible situation or scenario you will encounter in leadership. However, please remain on the lookout for my adult leadership book coming soon.

Thank you.
James C. Williams

77440616R00039

Made in the
USA
Columbia, SC